S. Smyth

T0t1Txt

The Big Bk of
Ltle Txt Msgs

With thanks to Gabrielle Mander
Compiled and edited by Philippa Wingate and David Sinden
Designed by Zoe Quayle
Cover design by Design 23

© Copyright Buster Books, 2001
First published in Great Britain in 2001 by Buster Books,
an imprint of Mary Ford Publications Ltd,
a subsidiary of Michael O'Mara Holdings,
9 Lion Yard, Tremadoc Road,
London SW4 7NQ, UK

A CIP catalogue record for this book is available from
the British Library

ISBN 1-903840-20-1

1 3 5 7 9 10 8 6 4 2

Visit our website at **www.mombooks.com**

Printed and bound in Finland by WS Bookwell, Juva

TOt1Txt

The Big Bk of
Ltle Txt Msgs

Buster Books

Contents

Calling all texters

Text messaging is the way smart people keep in touch. So don't be dumb, be a text maniac! Texting is a new language that uses letters, numbers, symbols and punctuation marks to create shorthand messages. It's a great way to send messages to friends using your mobile, a pager and by e-mail too.

Top secret

Texting is the ideal way to send secret information, because nobody can hear you when you type. We don't recommend it of course, but we understand that it has replaced passing notes as a way of making plans and exchanging gossip at the office or in the classroom.

It's cheap too

Text messaging is cheap for you and your friends. You won't spend hours on the phone chatting, and it's cheaper than typing messages in full. The fewer letters and spaces you use between words, the speedier and less expensive your messages are to send and receive.

Be safe

Text messaging is meant to be fun, but make sure it's safe too.

● Always make sure that you know the person you are sending a text message to, and never make arrangements to meet people you don't know, and that you have only met through text messaging.

● Text messaging is a cheap way to use your mobile phone, but don't get carried away and risk a huge telephone bill.

● Don't send really rude messages. People will know who they are from and, anyway, you should respect your friends.

Ready, steady, text...

It's easy to get texting. Although mobile phones vary, they all have a messaging service and it's simple to use.

Getting started

1. On your mobile's keypad, open the menu of options.
2. Scroll to "Messages" and select it.
3. In the Messages menu you will find an option called something like "Create" or "Message Editor".
4. When you select this option, you should be ready to start typing your message.

Letters, symbols and numbers

Use the letters, numbers, symbols and punctuation marks shown on the keys to write your message. Each key represents more than one letter or symbol, and you can use both capital letters and little letters. You'll need to press a key repeatedly until the letter you want appears. When it does, press the # key to stop that letter flashing and to move on to the next letter.

Press OK to send your message.

Fun 4 fast talkers

Fun 4 fast talkers

People in a hurry use "acronyms". These are made up
of the first letters of words in well known phrases.
Here are some essential acronyms:

AAMOF   as a matter of fact

ADN   any day now

AFAIK   as far as I know

AKA   also known as

ASAP   as soon as possible

ATM   at the moment

BBL   be back later

BFN   bye for now

BION   believe it or not

BRB   be right back

BTA   but then again

BTDT   been there, done that

BTW   by the way

CMB   call me back

ETA   estimated time of arrival

FICCL   frankly, I couldn't care less

GG good game

HAND have a nice day

IAC in any case

IDK I don't know

IMO in my opinion

IOOH I'm out of here

IOW in other words

IYDKIDKWD if you don't know,
I don't know who does

IYKWIM if you know what I mean

IYSS   if you say so

LMK   let me know

LOL   laughing out loud

MFI   mad for it

MYOB   mind your own business

NAGI   not a good idea

OTOH   on the other hand

PAW   parents are watching

PCM   please call me

SAL   such a laugh

TMB   text me back

TTFN   ta ta for now

TTYL   talk to you later

TYVM   thank you very much

WFM   works for me

YKWYCD you know what you can do

YYSSW   yeah, yeah, sure, sure, whatever

Teach yourself txt tlk

Teach yourself txt tlk

The trick to texting is to use as few letters and spaces as possible. It's all about creating short cuts. So, remember, keep it brief.

Tips and tricks

Here are some tips and tricks for creating your own text messages:

● Start each new word with a capital letter.

● Make words as short as you can. For example, "weekend" becomes **Wknd**, "forward" becomes **Fwd**.

● Why use a word when a letter or number will do? For example, in text talk "you" becomes **U** and "later" becomes **L8r**.

● A capital letter in the middle of a word can mean a double letter, so "bubble" becomes **BuBl**.

● A double "s" can be written like this **$**.

● A capital letter in the middle of a word can mean a long sound in a word. For example, the long "a" sound in "baby" becomes **BAB**, whereas the short "a" sound in "baggage" is written **BaGge**.

● Remember, you are the boss, so you can make up your own special abbreviations. For example, in this book the following special abbreviations have been made in the joke sections:

> **?UGt** means "what do you get?"
> **?UCALA** means "what do you call a?"

● You can even use a picture instead of letters to make sure your messages are as short as possible. For example "knock, knock" becomes **''[.** because it looks a little like two knocks on a door with a door handle. Throughout the book you will find many examples of pictures you can make from punctuation marks.

Txt tlk is easier than it sounds, and practice will make you the fastest texter around.

Texters' essentials

Here are some essential short cuts and abbreviations for texters:

B   be

BCNU   be seeing you

Bwd   backward

B4   before

C   see

ChLYa!   chill ya!

CU   see you

CUL8r   see you later

Fwd   forward

F2F   face to face

F2T   free to talk

Gr8   great

Gonna   going to

IH8U   I hate you

IU2U   it's up to you

K   a thousand

LkIt like it

Luv love

L8 late

L8r later

Mob mobile

Msg message

M8 mate

NE any

NE1 anyone

NO1   no one

Nt2Nite   not tonight

N1!   nice one!

OIC   oh, I see

On4It   on for it

Pls   please

R   are

RUOK?   are you OK?

RUThr?   are you there?

RUTlkn2Me?   are you talking to me?

RUUp4It?   are you up for it?

Sec   second

ST2MoRo   same time tomorrow

Sum1   someone

TA4N   that's all for now

ThnQ   thank you

Thnx   thanks

U   you

Up4It   up for it

UR   you are

Wan2   want to

Wan2Tlk?   want to talk?

W/   with

Wknd   weekend

W8   wait

W84Me   wait for me

X   cross

XLnt   excellent

Ya   you, or your

1daful   wonderful

2   to, or too

2day   today

2moRo   tomorrow

2nite   tonight

24/7   twenty-four hours a day, seven days a week

W8rW8r
Waiter, waiter

Waiter, waiter, what's wrong with this fish?
W8rW8r WotsRongW/ThsFsh?

Long time, no sea.
LngTImNoC

Waiter, waiter, do you have frog's legs?
W8rW8r DoUHveFrgsLgs?

No, I always walk like this.
NoIAlwAsWlkLlkThs

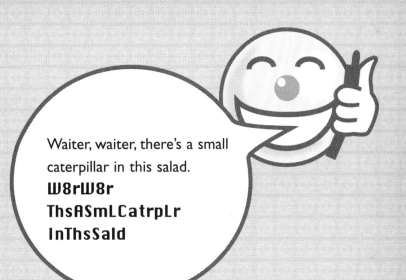

Waiter, waiter, there's a small caterpillar in this salad.
W8rW8r ThsASmLCatrpLr InThsSald

Would you like me to get you a bigger one?
WldULIKMe2GetUA BGa1?

Waiter, waiter, this egg is bad.
W8rW8r ThsEGIsBd

Don't blame me,
I only laid the table.
DntBlAmMe
IOnlELAdTTble

Waiter, waiter, there's a fly in my wine.
**W8rW8r
ThrsAFlyInMyWin**

You asked for something with a little body in it.
**UAskd4Sumn
W/ALTleBdyInIt**

Waiter, waiter, my lunch is talking to me.
W8rW8r MyLnchIsTlkn2Me

Well you did ask for a tongue sandwich.
WeLUDidAsk4ATung Sndwch

38

Emoticons

Emoticons

When you talk to your friends they can see from your face whether you are happy, sad or joking. Tell them you never want to see them again while winking and they will know you probably don't mean it. When you are talking to them on the phone, the tone of your voice helps them guess your mood.

Say it like you mean it

It's harder for people to tell what mood you are in from a text message. So texters use "emoticons" to show what they're feeling. These are faces made from the letters, numbers, symbols and punctuation marks that you'll find on your keyboard.

Put emoticons at the end of sentences to indicate how you're feeling. They take up very little space, can be keyed in seconds, and they could make the difference between a lasting friendship and all-out war.

The basic smiley face emoticon :-) is made from a colon, a dash and a close bracket. When you turn it 90° to the right, it becomes a smile.

Face it

On the following pages you will find some basic emoticons to use in your messages. Some have more than one meaning, so it depends on what you use them for. On pages 44 - 46 you will see a selection of emoticons especially for people wanting to text message jokes.

Don't panic!

If your phone doesn't have all the symbols and punctuation marks used in this book, don't panic. You will probably have most of them, and your computer keyboard will have all of them, so you can use them when you want to send e-mails (see page 194).

:-)   I'm smiling, or happy

;-)   I'm winking, or joking

:-D   I'm laughing

:'-(I'm crying

:-''''(now I'm really upset

:'-D   I'm crying with laughter

:-(I'm sad, or disappointed

:-C   now I'm really sad

:-I   I couldn't care less

:-*	I'm clowning around
I-o	I'm bored now
:-o	oops!
:=(	I've got two noses!
:_(	someone just punched me on the nose
.-(	I've lost a contact lens
:-Ш	I'm lying, speaking with a forked tongue
>;-)	I just had an evil thought
:-P	bleahhhh! (tongue sticking out)

Emoticons for jokers

If you are texting jokes to friends, emoticons can have different meanings. Here are some emoticons especially for jokers. (Find out what "full on" means on page 53.)

:-)))   ha ha ha

;-)   nice one

C=:-)   laughing my head off

+-:-O   dying laughing

:-@   shrieking with laughter

_/<   falling off my chair

:/)   cracking up

',-O.....   wetting myself

#:+)   I'm in stitches

,^)___S:-) tickled pink

:-OO   you're such a hoot

:-'''!   smokin'

:^,)"   a fit of the giggles

;-,   snigger

;^g   grinning

;^)@"   rolling on the floor

::--))   doubled up with laughter

(-.-)   a side splitter (full on)

(*_*)   beaming (full on)

0_*__*_0   grinning from ear to ear (full on)

0 @@ 0   heard it before (full on)

<:-l   dumb joke

[* _ *]

;^l+)   no laughing matter

;^l/)   having a humour bypass

46

Madicons

Once you've mastered the basics, you can add to and combine emoticons. There are no limits....
Do you recognize these faces?

~(_8^(I)   Homer Simpson

@@@@8-)   Marge Simpson

[@@@@8-) Marge Simpson
          with a Walkman

3:-)   Bart Simpson

{8-)   Lisa Simpson

[8-*   Maggie Simpson

Who's calling?

.o+I(=:   a ballerina

+-(:-)>+   the Pope

:-[a vampire

0:-)   an angel

0:-[Angel from "Buffy the Vampire Slayer"

:-E   a buck-toothed vampire

+<#^U   a knight

..._(:)-)   a scuba diver

... _( )-(a scuba diver with a broken mask

-(D)   an astronaut

*<:-)   Santa Claus

3:*>   Rudolph the Rednosed Reindeer

Cartoon callers

{:<>	Daffy Duck
8(:-)	Mickey Mouse
:----)	Pinnochio
7:n)	Fred Flintstone
~8-)	Harry Potter
>8o!...	Bugs Bunny with carrot
IIII8^)X	The Cat in the Hat
(*-*)	Pokémon

(o^-^o)   Pikachu (full on)

(((-_-)))   Cartman (full on)

(((> <)))   Kenny (full on)

[:=I]   Frankenstein

(>:[X   Count Dracula

]B-)   Batman

Out of this world

(-o-)   an Imperial TIE Fighter (full on)

>>>:-1   a Klingon

-\\/ /   the Klingon salute (full on)

/:-I   Mr. Spock

=-0   the starship Enterprise (full on)

=-0 * * *   the Enterprise firing photon
             torpedoes (full on)

=-0~~~~   the Enterprise firing phasers (full on)

:-)~~~~~<   "Beam me up, Scotty!"

Full on

Some emoticons can be viewed front on.

(-_-)   this is me

(>_<)   I'm angry

(=_=)   I'm sleepy

(*_*)   I'm falling in love

(@_@)   boggle-eyed

(((o-o)))   I've got my hood up

'\=o-o=/'   I'm wearing glasses

(^0^)   I'm singing joyously

(^.^)/   waving hello

(;.;)/~   waving goodbye

~// (^o^) /~/~ an octopus

@(*0*)@   a koala bear

(0υ0)   an owl

Hall of fame

/ :=(Adolf Hitler

cl:-=X   Charlie Chaplin

(0)   Posh Spice (full on)

(*0   Sporty Spice (full on)

(*0*)   Baby Spice (full on)

%%0%%   Scary Spice (full on)

             Ginger Spice (full on)

c8<]   Darth Vader

55

5:-)   Elvis

:-.)   Marilyn Monroe, or Cindy Crawford

8(:-) 8   Britney Spears as a Mousekateer

//0-0   John Lennon (full on)

?:^[]   Jim Carrey, Ace Ventura

Animal magic

:@)   a pig

}:-o   a cow

<:3)~~~   a mouse (full on)

})l([a butterfly (full on)

>-^);>   a fish (full on)

{:U   a duck

>-8~~~~~~ a snake (full on)

>-8888oooo))))   a rattlesnake (full on)

Off the wall

_____m_oLo_m__
a person spying over a wall

_____m_____m____
a very short person spying over a wall

__m__oLo__?__
Captain Hook spying over a wall

__\/_oo_\/_
a crab spying over a wall

_____,_____
an ant on a wall

_____2_____
a duck on a wall

____2_22222__
a duck and her ducklings on a wall

—,,,^..^,,,—
a cat looking over a wall

Whoa, bad hair day!

#:-(I just woke up like this

}:-(I've got a serious centre parting

?:-U   I've parted my hair on the right

=:-(the hairdresser gave me a Mohican haircut

,:-(I've just had a really serious haircut

(:-o   I've been scalped!

~-)   my fringe grew too long

{(:-)   I'm wearing a toupee

Fashion crime

d:-) I'm wearing a baseball cap

q:-) I'm wearing a baseball cap backwards

X<:-) I'm wearing a propeller-head beanie

*<o'υ I'm wearing a bobble hat (profile)

@:-) I'm wearing a turban

<<<<<|:-) I couldn't decide which hat to wear so I wore them all

8-) I'm wearing goggles

-) I should have worn goggles!

:-)#   I'm wearing a false beard

[:-)   I'm wearing a Walkman

]-)   I'm wearing sunglasses

B-)   I'm wearing cheap sunglasses

(B:-)   I'm wearing cheap sunglasses on my head

P-(my sunglasses are so cheap they broke

%-(now my sunglasses are completely broken

:-)K~   I'm wearing a tie

;-)K/////Ҡ> I'm wearing a really loud tie

YDdT8^xTRd?

Why did the chicken cross the road?

Why did the chicken cross the road?
YDdT8^xTRd?

To get to the other side.
2Gt2TOthaSId

Why did the chicken cross the road twice?
YDdT8^xTRd2yys?

Because he was a dirty double-crosser.
BcosHeWosADrtyDblexr

Why did the cow cross the road?
YDdT3:-oxTRd?

To get to the udder side.
2Gt2TUDrSld

Why did the turkey cross the road?
YDdT<:>==xTRd?

To prove he wasn't chicken.
2PrOvHWosnt8^

Why did the dinosaur cross the road?
YDdTDnsrxTRd?

Because chickens hadn't evolved yet.
Bcos8^sHdntEvlvdYt

Why did the chicken surf the net?
YDdT8^SrfTNet?

To get to the other site.
2Gt2TOthaSIt

Why did the chicken cross
the playground?
YDdT8^xTPlAgrnd?

To get to the other slide.
2Gt2TOthaSLld

Why did the chewing gum cross the road?
YDdTChwnGmxTRd?

Because it was stuck to the chicken.
BcosItWosStk2T8^

Why didn't the chicken cross the road?
YDdntT8^xTRd?

Because he lost his guts.
BcosHLstHsGuts

?UGt
What do
you get?

What do you get if you cross
a spider with a computer?
?UGt IfUxASpdrW/ACmputa

A web page.
AWebPAg

What do you get if you cross
a chicken with a monster?
?UGt IfUxA8^W/AMnsta

Free strange eggs.
FrEStrAngEGs

What do you get if you cross
 a bridge with a car?
?UGt IfUxABrdgW/ACA

To the other side of the river.
2TOthaSIdOfTRiva

What do you get if you cross
a kangaroo with a sweater?
?UGt IfUxAKngrOW/ASweta

A wooly jumper.
AWOlyJmpa

What do you get if you cross a car park with a safari park?

?UGt IfUxACAPrkW/ASfriPrk

Double yellow lions.

DbleYloLions

What do you get if you cross a
sheep with a radiator?
?UGt IfUxAShEpW/ARAdiata

Central bleating.
CntrIBIEtin

What do you get if you cross a
skunk with a table-tennis bat?
?UGt
IfUxASkunkW/ATblTeNisBt
Pong pong.
PongPong

What do you get if you cross
a skeleton with a dog?
?UGt IfUxASkItonW/ADg

An animal that buries itself.
AnAnmIThtBerEsItsIf

What do you get if you cross
a mouse with an olive?
?UGt IfUxAMseW/AnOliv

A squeak that oils itself.
ASqEkThtOilsItslf

What do you get if you cross
a toadstool with a wardrobe?
?UGt IfUxATdstOIW/AWrdrOb

Not mushroom for your clothes.
NtMushrOm4YaClOths

What do you get if you cross
a computer with a potato?
?UGt IfUxACmputaW/APtato

Microchips.
Mcrochps

What do you get if you cross
a cow with a map?
?UGt IfUxA3:-oW/AMap

Udderly lost.
UDrIELst

What do you get if you cross
a zebra with a pelican?
?UGt IfUxAZbraW/APeliCn

Across the street safely.
AxTStrEtSAfly

What do you get if you cross
a biscuit with a truck?

?UGt IfUxABscitW/ATruc

Crumbs.

Crmbs

Hot4U

Hot for you

Hot4U

For anyone smooching their honey, here's a mixture of acronyms, abbreviations and emoticons to keep you loved up.

AML   all my love

Bf   boyfriend

BGWM   be gentle with me

CSThnknAU   can't stop thinking about you

CUL8r   see you later

CW2CU   can't wait to see you

4EvrYrs   forever yours

Gf girlfriend

GGFN gotta go for now

GMTA great minds think alike

GrOvBAB! groovy baby!

HDEpIYLuv? how deep is your love?

HOHILuv head over heels in love

HotLuv hot love

Hot4U hot for you

HotX3 (feeling) hot, hot, hot

H&Ks — hugs and kisses

ICWenUXMe** — I see stars when you kiss me

IJC2SaILuvU — I just called to say I love you

ILuvU — I love you

ILuvUMED — I love you more each day

IMBLuv — it must be love

IOHiis4U — I only have eyes for you

IOWan2BWU — I only want to be with you

IWanU — I want you

IWLAlwysLuvU I will always love you

KOTC a kiss on the cheeks

KOTL a kiss on the lips

LuvYa love you

OBAB oh baby

PM private message

QT cutie

SRy sorry

SWALK sent with a loving kiss

TOY thinking of you

TruLuv true love

TTYL8r talk to you later

URT1 you are the one

U+Me=Luv you + me = love

WYWH wish you were here

X kiss

XMeQk kiss me quick

XOXOX hugs and kisses

:-*   I am sending you kisses

((name))   hug

(((((((name)))))))   big hug

(:-*   wish we were kissing

:-()-:   give me a snog

:-X   I'm sending you a big wet kiss

<3   I love you (heart)

:-p :-q :-p :-q

       I'm licking my lips at the thought
       of seeing you (sequence)

@}-->--   a rose

:-)(-:   best friends

:-{}-:   special friends

:-)I(-:   I love myself (looking in mirror)

:-) (-: + :-o o-: + :-p d-:
                   serious kissing (sequence)

IH8U
I hate you

IH8U

Don't get mad, get even. Here are a mixture of acronyms, abbreviations and emoticons to help to you get your own back.

BItMe   bite me

CIO   cut it out

CrEp   creep

DngBt   dingbat

Drk   dork

EMS   eat my shorts

EtYa<3Out eat your heart out

FngusFAc fungus face

GAL get a life

GL get lost

GoBak2YaPlnt go back to your planet

KISS keep it simple, stupid

Kltz klutz

LMA leave me alone

SaDo saddo

ScZBg scuzzbag

TOrg toe-rag

:-%(% you have a spot problem

(::::[]::::) you should put a plaster over your spots

>[:-) you watch too much TV, get a life!

:-))) you've got a fat face

:-)~ you dribbling idiot

:-)~~~0 you dribble so much you've made a puddle

::-)   four-eyes

+-)   you're cross-eyed

:^)   you've got a big nose

:/\)   you've got a really big nose

:0)   whoa! that's some nose

:~(who broke your nose?

:-(=)   you've got goofy teeth

:-(#)   I love your braces

l:-)   you should pluck your eyebrows

?UCALA
What do you call a?

What do you call a man with no underpants?
?UCALA MnW/0Undrpnts

Nicholas.
Nicolas

What do you call a friend with an elephant on his head?
?UCALA FrndW/An6U)OnHsHed

A flatmate.
AFlatmAt

What do you call a failed lion tamer?
?UCALA FAldLionTmr

Claude Bottom.
ClaudBoTm

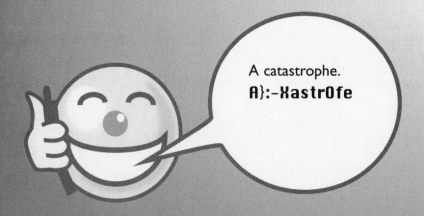

What do you call a sheep that says Quack?
?UCALA ShEpThtSezQak?

Bilingual.
Bilngwl

What do you call a woman crossing a river?
?UCALA WmnxnARivr

Bridget.
Brdgt

What do you call a small parent?
?UCALA SmLPArnt

A minimum.
AMniMm

What do you call a pen with no hair?
?UCALA PenW/NoHair

A bald point.
ABldPnt <:-)

What do you call a lady in the distance?
?UCALA LdyInTDstnce

Dot.
Dot

Knock, knock   "[.

Who's there?   .[?

Seymour   **Seymour**

Seymour who?   **SeymourHO?**

Seymour if you look through
the window.

SeymourIfULOkThrUTWndw

Knock, knock **"[.**

Who's there? **.[?**

Albert **Albert**

Albert who? **AlbertHO?**

Albert you'll never guess.
AlbertULNvrGe$

Knock, knock   ″[.

Who's there?   .[?

Stan   **Stan**

Stan who?   **StanHO?**

Stan back, I'm going to
break the door down.
                StanBckImGoNaBrkTDOrDwn

Knock, knock ”[.

Who's there? .[?

Luke **Luke**

Luke who? **LukeHO?**

Luke through the
keyhole and you'll see.
LukeThruTKEhle&ULC

Knock, knock   "[.

Who's there?   .[?

De Niro   **DeNiro**

De Niro who?   **DeNiroHO?**

De Niro you get, the
uglier you look.

DeNiroUGtTUgIrULOk

Freestyle

Freestyle

Here are some far-fetched, fantasy emoticons.

:'---(I'm sad because I have a big nose

:-D*   I'm laughing so hard I didn't notice a
                5-legged spider crawling up my lip

>]}   a dragon wearing sunglasses

>8-0-(&)<   the doctor just told me I've got an
                alien in my stomach

}:^#})   I'm happy even though my toupee
                is blowing off, and I have a bushy
                moustache, a pointy nose and a
                double chin

@@@@:-{)   Marge Simpson with a moustache

(XØIII)   get me a double burger with lettuce and tomato, please

(-::-)   Siamese twins

~oE]:-I   a fishseller with a basket on his head containing a three-legged octopus that is giving off smell rays

>:-[--<9   a girl who has found a squirrel climbing up her skirt

c=};-{Ø))   a chef with a wig in an updraft, a moustache and a double chin

@:-[a vampire wearing a turban

}:~#})   a person with a bushy moustache,
              an ugly nose and a double-chin

{I^x~   someone with a severe centre parting,
              kissing and dribbling

<'-?   someone with one winking eye, who
              is smoking a pipe

:-):-)   déjà vu

:U:-I   someone who doesn't realize there
              is an alligator on her head

[B-~[a vampire with a Walkman, sunglasses
              and a bad cold

SpOKE
Spooky

What do you call a ghost's father and mother?
?UCALA GOstsPa&Ma?

Transparents.
TransPArnts

What roads do ghosts
live on?
WotRdsDoGOstsLivOn?

Dead ends.
DedEnds

What position do ghosts play in football?
WotPositnDoGOstsPlAInFOtbL?

Ghoulie.
GhooLE

127

What did the ghost say to her son?
WotDidTGOstSA2HrSn?

Don't spook until you're spooken to.
DntSpOkUntIURSpOkn2

What flavour ice cream
do vampires like?
**WotFlAVaIcCrEmDo
:-i=sLlk?**

Veinilla.
VeiniLa

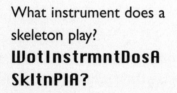

What instrument does a skeleton play?
WotInstrmntDosA SkltnPlA?

Trombone.
Trmbone

Who does a vampire fall in love with?
HODosA:-1=FLInLuvW/?

The girl necks door.
TGrlNeksDOr

Why didn't the skeleton go
to the party?
YDdntTSkltnGo2TParT?

She had no body to
go with.
SheHdNoBdy2GoW/

What did the skeleton say to her boyfriend?
WotDdTSkltnSA2HrBf?

I love every bone in your body.
ILuvEvrEBOnInYaBodE

How do you make a milkshake?
HowDoUMAkAMilkshAk?

Sneak up behind it and say "Boo!"
SnEkUpBhndIt&SABO!

Why are ghosts afraid?
YRGOstsAfrd?

Because they've got no guts.
BcosThyvGtNoGuts

Why do demons like ghouls?
YDoDmonsLkeGOls?

Because demons are a ghoul's best friend.
BcosDmonsRAGOls BstFrnd

When can't you bury people in a graveyard?
WenCntUBerEPpleInA GrAvyd?

When they're not dead.
WenThyRNtDed

Why are graveyards
always noisy?
YRGrAvydsAlwysNoisE?

Because of the coffin.
BcosOfTCoFn

Dnsrs

Dinosaurs

What followed the dinosaurs?
WotFLwdTDnsrs?

Their tails.
TherTAls

What's as big as a dinosaur
but weighs nothing?
WotsAsBgAsADnsrBtWAs0?

Its shadow.
ItsShdw

What do you get when you
cross a dinosaur with a bomb?
?UGt
WenUxADnsrW/ABom

Dinomite.
DnOmIte

What does a Tyrannosaurus eat?
WotDosATiraNosrusEt?

Anything she wants to.
NEthngSheWans2

What should you do if you find
a dinosaur in your bed?
WotShldUDoIfUFndADnsrInYaBd?

Sleep somewhere else.
SlEpSumwerEls

Do you know how long dinosaurs
walked the planet?
DoUNoHwLngDnsrsWlkdTPlnt?

Exactly the same as short dinosaurs.
XactLTSAmAsShrtDnsrs

What do you get if you cross
a dinosaur with a pig?
?UGt IfUxADnsrW/A:@)

Jurassic Pork.
Jra$icPork

What do you call a dinosaur who's
been left in the rain?
?UCALA DnsrHOsBnLftInTRAn

A Stegosaurust.
AStgosrust

Why do dinosaurs eat raw meat?
YDoDnsrsEtRwMEt?

Because they don't know how
to cook.
BcosThyDntNoHw2COk

What do you call a dinosaur
with no eyes?
?UCALA DnsrW/Øiis

A Doyouthinkhesaurus.
ADoYaThnkHeSrUs

149

What does a Triceratops
sit on?
WotDsATrcratpsSitOn?

Its Tricera-bottom.
ItsTrcraBoTm

Why are there old dinosaur bones
in the museum?
YRTherOldDnsrBnesInTMusEm?

Because they can't afford
new ones.
BcosThyCntAFrdNu1s

151

What do you get when a
dinosaur sneezes?
?UGt WenADnsrSnEzs

Out of the way.
OutOfTWA

How do you know if there's a dinosaur
in your refrigerator?
**HowDoUNoIfThersADnsr
InYaFrdge?**

Look for footprints in the pizza.
LOk4FOtprntsInTPiZa

2CO14SkO1

Too cool for school

Did you hear about the
cross-eyed teacher?
DdUHErAbtTxiidTecha?

She couldn't control her pupils.
SheCldntCntrlHrPupls

Why did the dinner lady get an electric shock?

YDdTDNrLADGtAnEIctrcShk?

She stepped on a bun and a current went up her leg.

SheStePdOnABun&ACuRnt
WntUpHrLg

156

Why does my teacher wear sunglasses?
YDosMyTechaWerB-)?

Because I am so bright.
BcosImSoBrIt

What's the longest word?
WotsTLngstWrd?

Smiles — because there's a mile
between the first and last letters.
:-)s BcosThersAMIL
BtwEnT1st&LstLeTrs

Where is the best place for the
school sickroom?
WersTBstPlAc4TSkOlSckrOm?

Next to the canteen.
Nxt2TCntEn

159

What's the longest sentence?

WotsTLngstSntnce?

Life imprisonment.

LlfImprsnmnt

Be sure that you go straight home!
BSurThtUGoStr8HOm!

I can't, I live around the corner.
ICntILivArndTCrnr

Laugh and the class laughs
with you.
:-)))&TCIa$:-)))sW/U

But you get detention alone!
BtUGtDtntnAlOn!

What is the best way to get
straight 'A's?

WotsTBstWA2GtStr8As?

Use a ruler.

UsARlr

163

Who invented fractions?
HOInvntdFrctns?

Henry the 1/8.
HnryT8th

164

What's the difference between an American school and an English school?

WotsTDffrnceBtwEn AUSSkOl&AUKSkOl?

About 3000 miles.

Abt3KMILs

What's the difference between school gravy and frogspawn?

WotsTDFrnsBtwEnSkOl Grvy&Frgsporn?

Not a lot.

NtALt

What came after the Stone Age?

WotCAmAftaTStnAg?

The sausage.

TSosij

DrDr

Doctor, doctor

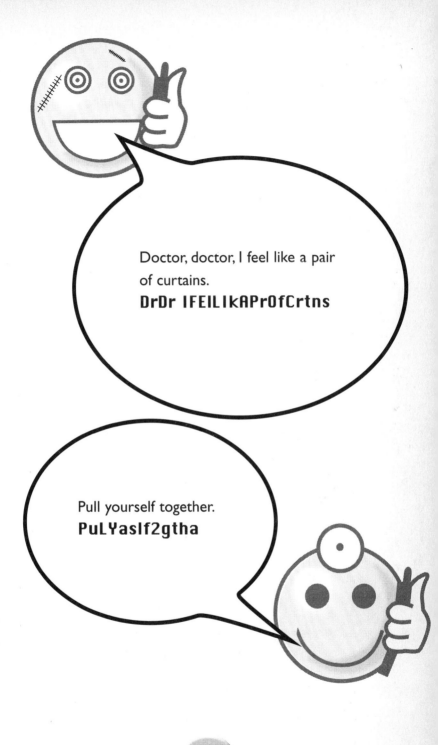

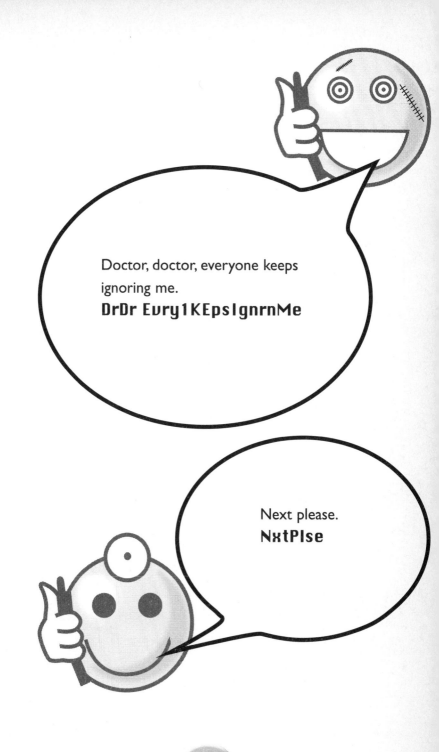

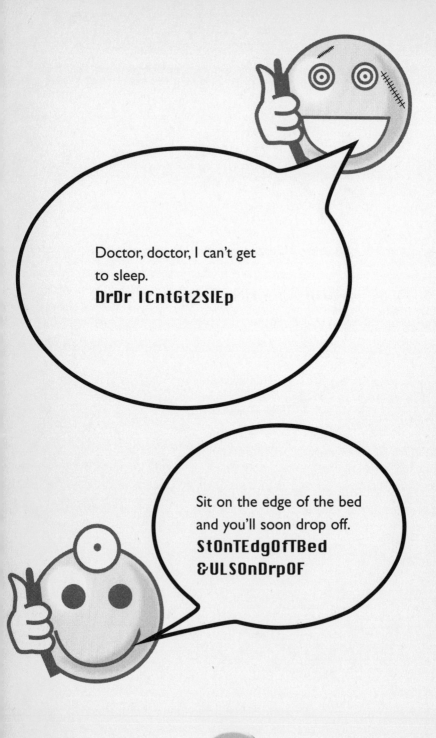

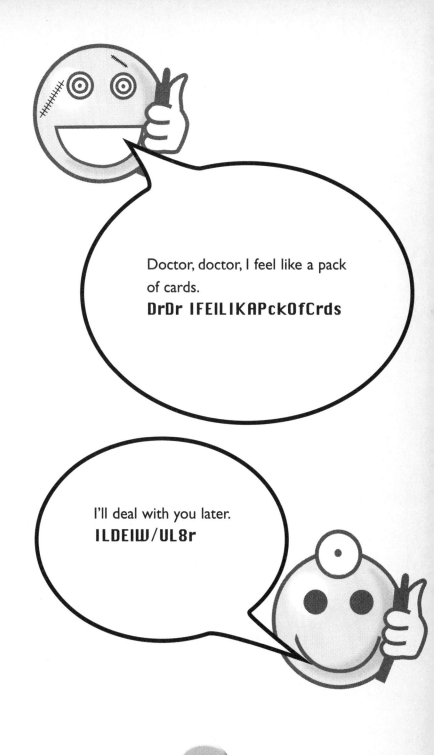

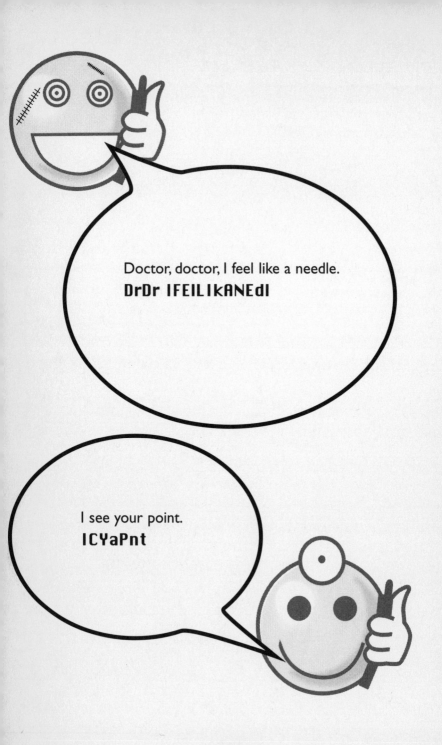

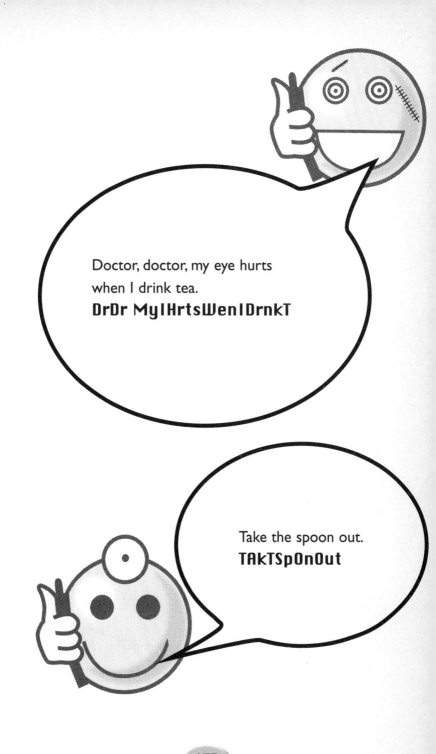

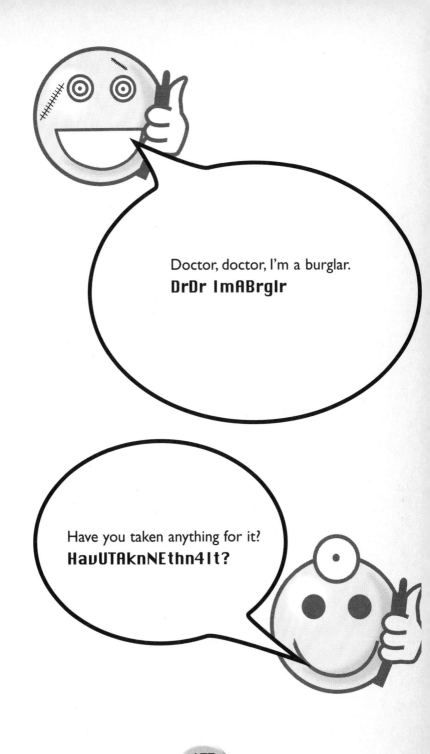

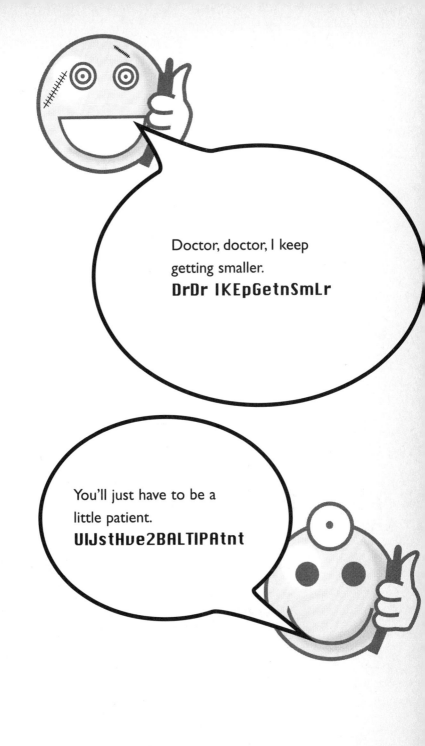

Signing off

Signing off

Once you've composed the perfect message, made your friends laugh, cry or cry with laughter, it's time to sign off. Develop your own personalized signature emoticon to add to all your messages.

How about doing "full body" emoticons like the ones below.

0=-<=   someone wearing a turtle neck sweater
             and a mini skirt

~oE]=   someone whose hair is standing up
             on end

@0-E<=   someone with their hair in a bun

B-)-[<   someone dressed for the beach in
             sunglasses and swimming trunks

:-0->-<   someone being held at gunpoint with
             their hands in the air

+]:)|->-<   the king of the universe

*|:^)(.)(...) love from Frosty the Snowman

(: (=   someone wearing a ghost costume

<|:-)->-<   someone ready to party in a party hat

-<:-o->-<   someone looking a bit stupid with
               a lampshade on their head

<:-)<<<<| someone who is on their way
               to the Moon

0-S-<   someone in a hurry

0-Z-<   someone in a big hurry

:-) >=>   a bookworm

__/\o_   a keen swimmer

o>8<l=   message for girls only

o....!!!! bye, I've gone bowling

=l>8<o

(...)(:)(>:l*

Ova2U
Over to you

Ova2U

Why not make up some of you own emoticons, acronyms and abbreviations, and jot them down on the following pages?

_____

_____

_____

_____

0va2U

_____

_____

_____

_____

_____

Ou2U

_____

_____

_____

_____

_____

_____

US2UO

_____

_____

_____

_____

_____

Ov a2U

Ova2U

_____

_____

_____

_____

_____

0va2U

192

0va2U

_____

_____

_____

_____

_____

Texters on the Net

Mobile phones are not the only means of sending text messages. On the Internet you can use txt tlk in lots of different ways. You can use all the acronyms, abbreviations and emoticons covered in this book in on-line chat of all kinds, including in e-mails and in chat rooms. Many websites offer free text messaging services with which you can send messages from your computer straight to someone's mobile phone.